THE REBUKE

OF

SECESSION DOCTRINES

BY SOUTHERN STATESMEN.

PHILADELPHIA:
PRINTED FOR GRATUITOUS DISTRIBUTION.
1863.

PATRIOTISM ABOVE PARTISANSHIP.

At a most enthusiastic meeting of the citizens of New York, attended, as it is estimated, by more than FIFTY THOUSAND citizens, Hon. JOHN VAN BUREN made a speech, from which we take the following passages:

THE UTTER CAUSELESSNESS OF THE REBELLION.

I heartily congratulate you upon this magnificent uprising of the people of the City of New York and the surrounding neighbourhood. It shows that there has been no abatement in that spirit of patriotism that distinguished the people of this country some two years since, on the first out-break of the rebellion, which has had no parallel in the civilized world. It is the first attempt on the part of men to upset a Government, when no man being engaged in that attempt was able, when it commenced, or has been at any time since, to name one single particular in which either his liberty, his property, or his life had been put in jeopardy No human being, whether he favoured the rebellion or whether he opposed it, has been able to understand how in any single regard those who attempted madly to overthrow the Government of this country had been in the slightest degree injured. I defy the talent and ingenuity of the most acute rebel in the Southern country, or any sympathizer with him, to tell me how he has been injured by the Government of this country up to this day. It was an utterly unjustifiable attempt to overthrow the existing Government. I have often conceded that there were circumstances of irritation—circumstances of provocation—but these constitute an excuse, not a justification. This rebellion is wholly without justification, in my judgment. This being the fact, it was natural for the people of this country to rise unanimously, as they did two years since, to put down the rebellion so unjustifiable, and in proof of that we assembled here, as other citizens in other portions of the United States have assembled, to declare to the constituted Government, whether it was an Administration of their own choice, or of their profession, that the time had come when party considerations must cease to operate, and when the people of this country with entire unanimity must uphold the Government of this country irrespective of all party considerations. I have entertained that opinion always, and although I did not address the meeting held two years since, I derived great gratification from the proceedings, and there never has been a moment from that time to this when I have seen anything to induce me to relax my efforts in upholding the Government and in putting down this rebellion. * * *

[*See third page of cover.*

THE REBUKE

OF

SECESSION DOCTRINES

BY

SOUTHERN STATESMEN.

PHILADELPHIA:
PRINTED FOR GRATUITOUS DISTRIBUTION.
1863.

NOTE.

In the following pages will be found four very remarkable and highly interesting documents,—

1. General Jackson's faithful reproof of the folly and madness of the Nullifiers in 1832.

2. The lament of that pure and highminded Statesman and Patriot, the late Hon. H. S. Legare, over the prospect and perpetration of the the same suicidal act by the people of his native City and State.

3. The extraordinary, but most true and unexaggerated exhibition of the causelessness and wickedness of the present Southern Rebellion, which Alexander H. Stephens made in his speech to the Georgia Convention. And

4. The Platform on which one of the Delegates to the National Democratic Convention, at Charleston, in the spring of 1860, proposed to harmonize all parties, and secure the peace of the country to the end of the world!

THE REBUKE OF SECESSION DOCTRINES.

On the 24th of November, 1832, a convention of delegates met at Charleston, South Carolina, passed an ordinance to "provide for arresting the operation of certain acts of the Congress of the United States, purporting to be laws laying duties and imposts on the importation of foreign commodities." On the 10th day of December, succeeding, ANDREW JACKSON, of Tennessee, then President of the United States, issued a proclamation, in which the following memorable sentences occur:

I consider the power to annul a law of the United States, assumed by one state, incompatible with the existence of the Union, contradicted expressly by the letter of the Constitution, unauthorized by its spirit, inconsistent with every principle on which it is founded, and destructive of the great object for which it was formed:

The President, in the same document, thus appeals to his fellow citizens who had countenanced this insurrectionary measure:

I have urged you to look back to the means that were used to hurry you on to the position you have now assumed, and forward to the consequences it will produce. Something more is necessary. Contemplate the condition of that country of which you still form an important part. Consider its government uniting in one bond of common interest and general protection so many different states, giving to all their inhabitants the good title of AMERICAN CITIZENS, protecting their commerce, securing their literature and their arts, facilitating their intercommunication, defending their frontiers, and making their name respected in the remotest parts of the earth. Consider the extent of its territory, its increasing and happy population, its advance in arts which render life agreeable, and the sciences which elevate the mind. See education spreading the lights of religion, humanity and general information, into every cottage in the wide extent of our territories and states. Behold it as the asylum where the wretched and the oppressed find a refuge and, support. Look on this picture of happiness and honour, and say, "WE TOO ARE CITIZENS OF AMERICA." Carolina is one of these proud states; her arms have defended, her best blood has cemented this happy Union. And then add, if you can, without horror and remorse, This happy Union we will dissolve, this picture of peace and prosperity we will deface, this free intercourse we will interrupt, these fertile fields we will deluge with blood, the protection of that glorious flag we renounce, the very name of Americans we discard. And for what, mistaken men! for what do you throw away these inestimable blessings? For what would you exchange your share in the advantages and honours of this Union? For a dream of a separate independence—a dream interrupted by bloody conflicts with your neighbours, and a vile dependence on a foreign power. If your leaders could succeed in establishing a separation, what would be your situation? Are you united at home? Are you free from the apprehension of civil discord with all its fearful consequences? Do our neighbouring republics, every day suffering some new revolution, or contending with some new insurrection,—do they excite your envy? But the dictates of a high duty oblige me solemnly to announce that you cannot succeed. The laws of the United States must be executed.

At the time these measures were in progress, the Hon. H. S. Legare, at one time Attorney General and acting Secretary of State of the United States, was abroad. Of his character and position as a man, a citizen, a scholar, a statesman and a pure patriot, it is superfluous to speak. The memory of few public men of any age or country is more fragrant than his. With deep concern he heard, while

"Wandering on a foreign strand,"

of the proceedings of the convention in his native city, and with characteristic promptness and ingenuousness he addressed a letter to a friend at home, from which the following paragraphs are taken:

OCTOBER 2, 1832.

So you are going to nullify. Well, I can't say I have any great confidence in men when they are wound up to the revolutionary pitch, but I strive to hope against hope. I trust in God that my glorious and happy country, a thousand times dearer to me now, and grander in my estimation by contrast than it ever was, is not about to seal forever the dismal doom of our miserable species. * * * If the Union should go to pieces it will be one hideous wreck, of which, excepting New England, no two parts will hold together. None of us will have any country, except a technical country, a legal right and a civil status to decide on a question of title. But there will be no *flag* known to the nations, and none of the ennobling and and sacred charities that bind, or rather bound us together but the other day. No proud retrospect of the past, no glowing anticipations of the future, but piratical depredations instead, and ignoble border warfare, and the rudeness, coarseness, and ferocity of a race of mounted barbarians, and all the calamities that have scourged this continent, without the chivalry that has adorned her valour, and the grandeur that has half excused the ambition it has excited. * * *

April 8, 1833.

But I shall be very much surprised, or rather (for I begin to be surprised at nothing at all which our orang-outang race perpetrates now-a-days) I shall be exceedingly indignant, or downcast, or both, if the fantastic tricks of wanton, cold-blooded tyranny which the Convention has played off before the world, to its deep and serious instruction in politics, do not yet awaken us all to the importance of the inquiry, whether that same "Sovereignty of the States," about which we are mouthing as much as the Carlists do about monarchy *jure divino*, and which experience has thus shown to be of precisely the same stamp; whether that same sovereignty isn't still, as it was at the beginning, much too strong, not only for purposes of good government, vulgarly so-called, but, to be at all consistent with the preservation of a very humble share of the liberties transmitted to us from our English forefathers, and meant to be maintained in their integrity by the revolution.

When I read your "Ordinance," I rubbed my eyes to be sure that I was not in a dream. I could not believe it possible that such insolent tyranny was in the heart of any man; educated as and where I myself imbibed my detestation of all arbitrary power, though its sceptre be in my own gripe. I don't speak of it as a federal or anti-federal measure—pass for that—I refer to it exclusively as a measure of government in South Carolina, and I declare to you solemnly, that, for the very first time during this whole controversy, I felt the spirit of civil war burning within me, and that I fervently prayed that my friends of the Union party would, without any hesitation, swear that it should never be enforced but at the point of the bayonet. What made it worse was that (if I have not quite forgotten the Constitution of the State) nothing is plainer than that the "Convention" was a mere self-constituted assembly—a mob, without a place or name in our laws—because the Legislature which called it was no legislature until the constitutional time of meeting in November.

But putting the matter of right altogether out of the question, as it seems to be in South Carolina under its new government, how could the leaders and their convention, knowing, as they must know, unless they are mad, the inherent weakness of the State and of the whole South, if civil war do take place in good earnest; how could they be blind to the wild impolicy of their conduct? They first practice, with the utmost deliberation, a fraud upon the people, by assuring them that their premeditated scheme of violence is a perfectly regular and peaceable one. They succeed in bringing over a bare majority of our people, even with this plausible pretence in their mouths. They know that out of 39,000 votes, upwards of 16,000 are against them in every view of the measure. And yet, holding so feeble a majority by such a tenure, they venture to pass an "Ordinance," of which I never can think, and, I suppose, none of my friends ever do think, without feeling that life under such a tyranny (if it could be enforced) is not worth having. If it had been designed as a measure of mere vengeance, if, believing they would be ultimately thwarted in their plan of resistance, and wishing to prevent the triumphant scoffings of the Union party at their anticipated discomfiture and disgrace, they had determined to exterminate, at least, to banish them all at once, which, as Milton's Satan says, if not victory, were, at least, revenge—*à la bonne heure*. But, if we suppose them to have been anything but a gang of desperadoes, (as they certainly were!—am I not liberal?) how can it be accounted for, except by that spirit of intoxication and wilfulness which is said to be the forerunner of the downfall of kings and principalities and powers?

A true Prophet but a false Man.

ALEXANDER H. STEPHENS was an earnest and staunch opposer of secession doctrines. He could not fail to see the inevitable consequences of the measure, though by a strange hallucination he afterwards covered his eyes, joined the infatuated company of conspirators against a government which he had just exonerated from all reproach, and leaped into the very abyss of which he had implored them to beware. Here in his speech, delivered in the convention called to determine if Georgia should secede, Mr. Stephens said:

That this step once taken, could never be recalled; and all the baleful and withering consequences that must follow, (as they would see,) will rest on the Convention for all coming time. When we and our posterity shall see our lovely South desolated by the demon of war which this act of yours will inevitably invite and call forth; when our green fields of waving harvests shall be trodden down by the murderous soldiery and fiery car of war sweeping over our land; our temples of justice laid in ashes; all the horrors and desolations of war upon us; who but this Convention will be held responsible for it? and who but he who shall have given his vote for this unwise and ill-timed measure, (as I honestly think and believe,) shall be held to strict account for this suicidal act, by the present generation, and probably cursed and execrated by posterity for all coming time, for the wide and desolating ruin that will inevitably follow this act you now propose to perpetrate?

Pause, I entreat you, and consider for a moment what reasons you can give that will even satisfy yourselves in calmer moments—what reasons you can give to your fellow-sufferers in the calamity that it will bring upon us? What reasons can you give to the nations of the earth to justify it? They will be the calm and deliberate judges in the case; and to what cause or *one* overt act can you name or point, on which to rest the plea of justification? What right has the North assailed? What interest of the South has been invaded? What justice has been denied? and what claim founded in justice and right has been withheld? Can either of you to-day name one govermental act of wrong, deliberately and purposely done by the government of Washington, of which the South has a right to complain? I challenge the answer! While, on the other hand, let me show the facts, (and believe me, gentlemen, I am not here the advocate of the North; but I am here the friend, the firm friend and lover of the South and her institutions, and for this reason I speak thus plainly and faithfully for *yours*, *mine*, and every other man's interest, the words of truth and soberness,) of which I wish you to judge, and I will only state facts which are clear and undeniable, and which now stand as records authentic in the history of our country.

When we of the South demanded the slave trade, or the importation of Africans for the cultivation of our lands, did they not yield the right for twenty years? When we asked a three-fifths representation in Congress for our slaves, was it not granted? When we asked and demanded the return of any fugitive from justice, or the recovery of those persons owing labour or allegiance, was it not incorporated in the Constitution, and again ratified and strengthened in the Fugitive Slave Law of 1850?

But do you reply that in many instances they have violated this compact, and have not been faithful to their engagements? As individuals and local communities they may have done so; but not by the sanction of government, for that has always been true to Southern interests. Again, gentlemen, look at another act: when we have asked that more territory should be added, that we might spread the institution of slavery, have they not yielded to our demands in giving us Louisiana, Florida and Texas, out of which four States have been carved, and ample territory for four more to be added in due time, if you by this unwise and impolitic act do not destroy this hope, and, perhaps, by it lose all, and have your last slave wrenched from you by stern military rule, as South America and Mexico were; or by the vindictive decree of a universal emancipation, which may reasonably be expected to follow?

But, again, gentlemen, what have we to gain by this proposed change of our relation to the general government? We have always had the control of it, and can yet, if we remain in it, and are as united as we have been. We have had a majority of the Presidents chosen from the South; as well as the control and management of most of those chosen from the North. We have had sixty years of Southern Presidents to their twenty-four, thus controlling the Executive department. So of the Judges of the Supreme Court, we have had eighteen from the South, and but eleven from the North; although nearly four-fifths of the judicial business has arisen in the Free States, yet a majority of the Court has always been from the South. This we have required so as to guard against any interpretation of the Constitution unfavorable to us. In like manner we have been equally watchful to guard our interests in the Legislative branch of government. In choosing the presiding Presidents (*pro tem.*) of the Senate, we have had twenty-four to their eleven. Speakers of the House, we have had twenty-three, and they twelve. While the majority of the Representatives, from their greater population, have always been from the North, yet we have so generally secured the Speaker, because he, to a great extent, shapes and controls the legislation of the country. Nor have we had less control in every other department of the general government. Attorney-Generals we have had fourteen, while the North have had but five. Foreign ministers we have had eighty-six, and they but fifty-four. While three-fourths of the business which demands diplomatic agents abroad is clearly from the Free States, from their greater commercial interests, yet we have had the principal embassies so as to secure the world-markets for our cotton, tobacco, and sugar on the best possible terms. We have had a vast majority of the higher offices of both army and navy, while a larger proportion of the soldiers and sailors were drawn from the North. Equally so of Clerks, Auditors, and Comptrollers filling the Executive department, the records show for the last fifty years that of the three thousand thus employed, we have had more than two-thirds of the same, while we have but one-third of the white population of the Republic.

Again, look at another item, and one, be assured, in which we have a great and vital interest; it is that of revenue, or means of supporting government. From official documents, we learn that a fraction over three-fourths of the revenue collected for the support of government has uniformly been raised from the North.

Pause now while you can, gentlemen, and contemplate carefully and candidly these important items. Look at another necessary branch of government, and learn from stern statistical facts how matters stand in that department. I mean the mail and Post-Office privileges that we now enjoy under the general government as it has been for years past. The expense for the transportation of the mail in the Free States was, by the report of the Post-Master General for the year 1860, a little over $13,000,000, while the income was $19,000,000. But in the Slave States the transportation of the mail was $14,716,000, while the revenue from the same was $8,001,026, leaving a deficit of $6,115,735, to be supplied by the North for our accommodation, and without it we must have been entirely cut off from this most essential branch of government.

Leaving out of view, for the present, the countless millions of dollars you must expend in a war with the North; with tens of thousands of your sons and brothers slain in battle, and offered up as sacrifices upon the altar of your ambition,—and for what, we ask again? Is is for the overthrow of the American government, established by our common ancestry, cemented and built up by their sweat and blood, and founded on the broad principles of *Right, Justice,* and *Humanity?* And, as such, I must declare here, as I have often done before, and which has been repeated by the greatest and wisest of statesmen and patriots in this and other lands, that *it is the best and freest government—the most equal in its rights—the most just in its decisions—the most lenient in its measures, and the most inspiring in its principles to elevate the race of men, that the sun of heaven ever shone upon.*

Now, for you to attempt to overthrow such a government as this, under which we have lived for more than three-quarters of a century—in which we have gained our wealth, our standing as a nation, our domestic safety while the elements of peril are around us, with peace and tranquillity accompanied with unbounded prosperity and rights unassailed—is the height of madness, folly and wickedness, to which I can neither lend my sanction nor my vote."

The object for which the Rebellion was planned and contrived.

Nowhere is this topic more ably treated than in the speech, delivered in the House of Representatives, January 31, 1863, by the Hon. Horace Maynard, of Tennessee. The following passages particularly are entitled to the closest attention of every man among us, who is sincerely desirous that this war may cease, and may be followed by a genuine and stable PEACE.

Another error on the part of some of our Northern friends, caused by a failure adequately to appreciate the controlling influences of the rebellion, consists in supposing that our troubles may be composed, and the contest adjusted by compromise. Let me again repeat, that the object of the rebel leaders is empire, dominion over a territory and a people that they can govern; and as incident to that, the destruction of the nation, whereof you are a part, and which on the 4th of July next, will want but thirteen years to have lived a century. *They* mean the death of the nation; *you* mean its life. There is nothing to compromise. One side or the other must *wholly* fail. The nation must either live or die. They know perfectly well that for them safety lies only in success. Short of that, no matter what compromise you make, nor what acts of amnesty you pass, if the Federal Union still survives under the Constitution of our fathers, they are ruined, driven into obscurity, and their names clothed with infamy. Hence they, through all their organs, spurn the idea of ever living more with you under the same Government. Though you should humble yourselves in terms the most abject, even going to them barefoot, with your arms pinioned and halters about your necks, they would not receive you into the crowd of their vassals. All your suggestions of an armistice and reconciliation only intensify their expressions of scorn and loathing. Says one of their organs:

"While the North begins to see the folly and impossibility of attempting to conquer the South, they are not yet ready to grant our just demands. They hope still to chain us by some specious compromise to the corpse of the old Union. We would not reunite with them if they would, one and all, consent to occupy the same position of degradation which they aimed to rivet on us. *We would not consent to hold the Northern States as provinces.*"—*Richmond Enquirer, January* 6.

Another indulges in these words:

"*If the whole Yankee race should fall down in the dust to-morrow and pray us to be their masters, we would spurn them even as slaves.* We are aware that many persons believe that the party of which Brookes and Van Buren are representatives, desire and design to restore peace. We do not believe they are in favor of any such thing. They would like peace on condition of our returning to the Union, and they are fools enough to believe that a majority of the people in the confederacy are in favor of reunion. They look only to their pockets when they talk of reconciliation and restoration. Anything but that. English colonization, French vassalage, Russian serfdom—all, all are preferable to any association with the Yankees."—*Richmond Dispatch, January* 10.

A third varies the language:

"We have committed many errors in our treatment of the Yankees. Not the least has been in regarding them as something better than they really are. They are by nature menials, and fitted only for menial duties. *They are in open and flagrant insurrection against their natural lords and masters, the gentlemen of the South.* In the exercise of their assumed privileges, they deport themselves with all the extravagant airs, the insolence, the cruelty, the cowardice, and love of ropine which have ever characterized the revolt of slaves. The former leniency of their masters only serves to aggravate the ferocity of their natures. When they are again reduced to subjection, and taught to know their place, we must take care to put such trammels about them that they will never have an opportunity to play these tricks again."—*Richmond Whig.*

Davis, their chieftain, in a late speech in Richmond, asks:

"For what are they waging war? They say, to preserve the Union. Can they preserve the Union by destroying the social existence of a portion of the South? Do they hope to reconstruct the Union by striking at everything which is dear to men? By showing themselves so utterly disgraced, that if the question was proposed to you, whether you would combine with hyenas or Yankees, I trust every Virginian would say, 'Give me the hyenas?'"

This, bear in mind, is said of your brothers and sons, whom he characterizes as "off-scourings of the earth," and whose career, especially in northern Mississippi, he asserts has been marked by "every crime conceivable, from the burning of defenceless towns to the stealing of silver forks and spoons."

It is impossible not to be amused at the simplicity of a New York politician, writing to one of the chief conspirators, as early as January, 1861. He says:

"I think South Carolina committed a grave error when she raised the Palmetto flag, to the exclusion of the stars and stripes. And she erred, too, when she fired on the latter from beneath the folds of the former. This was very impolitic. For God's sake, let the seceding States cling to the Constitution, cling to the national flag, and declare to the world that it is for the integrity of the former and the honor of the latter that they are found with arms in their hands. By doing this they will divide the North against itself, and succeed with tenfold ease. And so, whenever they seize a fort or arsenal, let the old flag still float from its summit—let it be asserted that those forts, &c., were erected for the defence of the States in which they stand, and that upon the citizens of these States, whose interests and lives are imperiled, should devolve the post of honor in the hour of danger; and that it is to save the honor of the flag, and secure the rights of the people, from the treasonable assertions of abolitionists, possession has been taken of the Federal fortifications.

"Let the South be discreet, and she has nothing to fear. Let it be rung out through the land, however, that she asks her constitutional rights only—security in the possession of property, equal and exact rights in all other respects. *Let her sons not jeopardize the safety of their Northern allies by committing wrongs or excesses.*"

There are hundreds through the North who, like this zealous partisan and ally of "the South," imagined that the rebellion originated in some right denied or endangered, or some wrong suffered or apprehended, and who, like him, deprecate the "impolitic" course of their "Southern brethren." It is difficult to resist the conviction that such persons have far more sympathy with rebels in arms against the nation's life, than with those Southern men who from the beginning have withstood them, and exposed their nefarious schemes.

The truth is, there lurks at the bottom of their conduct a conviction that the Union will be maintained, if not a determination that it shall be. Hence their eye upon the coming future, when it is supposed that these chief plotters will return to their vacant seats and wield their former power. That future neither your eyes nor mine will ever see. The South, redeemed and disenthralled from the despotism that so long has weighed like nightmare upon it, will resume its ancient place beneath the flag. But woe to the men who by falsehood and treachery and base corruption have betrayed it into war and its consequent horrors! Their day of power in the Government is past. Other men, of nobler mould and fairer name, will succeed to the places they so betrayed. They will sink deeper than ever plummet sounded, dragging with them all who, either from guilt, sympathy or interested hope, shall cling to their skirts. Truth, and her sister Vengeance, go hand in hand.

The Tie that bound the Southern Democracy to the North.

In the progress of the exciting scenes which attended the *Democratic National Convention* at Charleston, S. C., in 1860, things were said and done which are too significant in their bearing to be dropped out of sight. We well know how entirely metamorphosed an object becomes by changing the light in which it is viewed, and how a man will do and say in one place or company, what he would be quite ashamed to say elsewhere or at another time.

Among the speeches made at Charleston, was one by Mr. Gaulden of the Georgia delegation, giving his reasons for not joining his colleagues who had seceded from the convention. It discloses in a "free and easy" way, the political affiliations then existing, and their basis; and cannot fail to throw light upon the present duty of true Union men.

MR. GAULDEN "DEFINES HIS POSITION."

"I am a Southern States rights man," said Mr. G. "I am an African slave-trader. I am one of those Southern men who believe that slavery is right, morally, religiously, socially, and politically. I believe that the institution of slavery has done more for this country, more for civilization, than all other interests put together. I believe if it were in the power of this country to strike down the institution of slavery, it would put civilization back two hundred years. I believe that our government was a Confederation of States for certain specified objects with limited powers—that the domestic relations of each State are to be and should be left to themselves; that this eternal slavery question has been the bone of contention between the North and South, which if kept in the halls of Congress must break up this government."

As to the exclusion of slavery from the territories, Mr. Gaulden regarded it as a mere abstraction. "You have cut off the supply of slaves," he says. "You have crippled the institution of slavery in the States by your unjust laws. We have no slaves to carry into these territories. We can never make another slave State with our present supply of slaves. But if we could, it would not be wise, as it would only withdraw slaves from Maryland, Delaware, or Virginia, and to that extent make theirs free soil. * * * *

A SOUTHERN VIEW OF THE "TRUE UNION MAN."

"I would ask my friends of the South to come up in a proper spirit; ask our Northern friends to give us all our rights, and take off the ruthless restrictions which cut off the supply of slaves from foreign lands. As a matter of right and justice to the South, I would ask the democracy of the North to grant us this thing, and I believe they have the patriotism and honesty to do it, because it is right in itself. I tell you, fellow democrats, that the African slave-trader is the true Union man.

WHY VIRGINIA OPPOSED THE AFRICAN SLAVE-TRADE.

"I tell you that the slave-trading of Virginia is more immoral, more unchristian in every point of view, than that African slave-trade, which goes to Africa and brings a heathen and worthless man here, makes him a useful man, Christianizes him, and sends him and his posterity down the stream of time, to join in the blessings of civilization. Now, fellow democrats, so far as any public expression of the State of Virginia—the great slave-trading State of Virginia—has been given, they are all opposed to the African slave-trade. Now, gentlemen, we are told, upon high authority, that there is a certain class of men who strain at a gnat and swallow a camel. Now, Virginia which authorizes the buying of Christian men, separating them from their wives and children, from all the relations and associations amid which they have lived for years, rolls up her eyes in holy horror, when I would go to Africa, buy a savage, and introduce him to the blessings of civilization and Christianity. Now, fellow-democrats, the slave-trade of Virginia forms a mighty and powerful reason for its opposition to the African slave-trade, and in this remark I do not intend any disrespect to my friends from Virginia. Virginia the mother of States and of Statesmen—the mother of Presidents—I apprehend, may err as well as other mortals. I am afraid that her error in this regard lies in the promptings of the almighty dollar. It has been my fortune to go into that noble old State and buy a few darkies, and I have had to pay from $1000 to $2000 a head, when I could go to Africa and buy better negroes for $50 a piece. (great laughter.) Now it is unquestionably to the interest of Virginia to break down the African slave-trade, when she can sell her negroes at $2000. She knows that the African Slave-trade would break up her monopoly, and hence her objections to it. If any of you, Northern democrats, (for I have more faith in you than I have in the carpet-knight democracy of the South,) will go home with me to my plantation in Georgia, I will show you some darkies that I bought in Maryland, some that I bought in Virginia, some that I bought in Delaware, some in Florida, some in North Carolina, and I will also show you the pure African—the noblest Roman of them all. * * *

A SOUTHERN STATESMAN'S ONLY WAY TO SAVE THE COUNTRY.

"I come from the first congressional district of the State of Georgia. I represent the African Slave-trade interests of that section. I am proud of the position I occupy in that respect. I believe that the African Slave-trader is a true missionary and a true Christian, and I have pleaded with my delegation to put this issue squarely to the Northern democracy and say to them, Are you prepared to go back to first principles, and take off your unconstitutional restrictions, and leave this question to be settled by each State? Now do this, fellow citizens, and you will have peace in the country. But as long as your Federal Legislature takes jurisdiction of this question, so long will there be war, so long will there be ill-blood, so long will there be strife; and this glorious Union of ours shall be disrupted and go out in blood and night forever! I advocate a repeal of the laws prohibiting the slave-trade, because I believe it to be the true Union movement. I do not believe that sections whose interests are so different as the Southern and Northern States, can ever stand the shocks of fanaticism unless they be equally balanced. I believe by re-opening this trade and giving us negroes to populate the territories, that the equilibrium of the two sections will be maintained. Then, gentlemen, we should proceed harmoniously, go on to prosper and prospering until the last trump of God should sound—until time was merged in the ocean of eternity." Thus far Mr. Gaulden.

But Northern Democracy was made of too stern stuff to yield to the persuasive words of the Georgia Slave-trader. There were those, undoubtedly, whose interest in sustaining a party policy was deep enough to have secured their acceptance of his startling proposition. But the demand was too bald—the leap too appalling for men of free sympathies and associations. Had the Democratic party yielded to Southern dictation in 1860, John C. Breckenridge would have been where Mr. Lincoln is, with an appropriate cabinet. The slave-holding interest would have remained in the ascendant. Cotton would have been abundant and cheap; the manufacturers of Lancashire would have been heaping up gold; and though English shipwrights would have lost the opportunity to furnish a fleet of war-ships for the "Emperor of China," and the English Government the opportunity to illustrate their idea of "Neutrality," and though the English people could still have twitted us about the significant "stripes" in our national banner, England herself could have claimed a position in American eyes which she has now lost and will never regain.

Because the North and West would not adopt the Southern policy, nor consent to the extension of involuntary servitude beyond its then present limits, nor yield to the dictation of a minority, this unnatural and ferocious rebellion was undertaken. Let our fellow-citizens and fellow-men understand that *our government is engaged not in a war against slavery, but in suppressing an insurrection in behalf of slavery and the slave-trade!*

MODE OF PUTTING DOWN THE REBELLION.

Fellow-citizens, allow me to say a few words to you about the mode of putting down this rebellion. I do not believe that simply belonging to the Democratic party will end the war that has been going on these two years. Since I belonged to the party, JEFF. DAVIS claimed to be a member, so does MASON and SLIDELL. I do not see that that ends the war. What would be thought of the passengers of a ship, who in a dreadful gale found that the vessel had sprung aleak, and who should say to others, "Find out where the leak is; stop it at all hazards; if our masts are all carried away, rig a jury-mast; if you can't save the ship save the passengers; construct a raft; be sure and save our lives, and as for the rest we will sit here and grumble; we belong to the Democratic party." If that ship had to be lightened to be saved it is easy to see what part of the cargo ought to be thrown overboard. * * *

THE GRAND QUESTION AT THE PRESENT MOMENT.

The interesting inquiry to this generation, in the present crisis, is what they are to do now. And now there is but one thing to do—that is, to fight. Did anybody ever hear, that when people make war upon you, you are to supplicate for peace? Why, if we are conquered, of course we must sue for peace; but if we are not conquered, then all we have to do is to fight. Suppose a man came up to you and took you by the throat, would you call upon your friends to see upon what terms he would settle? I know of no way except to defend yourself, and defend yourself by assailing him, and assailing him in his most vulnerable part, keeping always in mind the practice of the early Christians, and keeping as near the rules of civilized warfare as the circumstances will permit. Now, fellow-citizens, let us look for a few moments—and I will detain you but a very few minutes—at the conditions of this war. Let us see whether there is anything to discourage us in what has occurred. I say there is everything to encourage the people of the loyal States, taking a proper and rational view of the circumstances of the country. We were a people of peace two years ago; we knew nothing of war waged upon a great scale, in which the whole nation should be involved. We have recovered a very large portion of the territory of the United States—we have recovered a large portion of Tennessee, nearly the whole of Kentucky, a large portion of Louisiana, nearly the whole of Virginia, and very large districts of the country; we have preserved a blockade for two years; and I have entire confidence that if there was not a blow struck for twelve months, if this blockade could be preserved for the twelve months, the rebellion would be subdued. I don't desire to wring a victory from the pinched bellies of that people, in preference to extracting it from their battered heads; but there is no doubt that if this blockade is vigorously preserved, as now, and it is certain that it can be, for the next twelve months, the war will be ended. * * *

It is impossible that this controversy can have but one result; it is

[*See fourth page of cover.*

impossible that it can be protracted any great-length of time, if we are a united people; and to be a united people we must discard political considerations. Why, have not we as much patriotism as the Southern people, and did you ever hear of a contested election there during this rebellion? Who ran against JEFFERSON DAVIS? What one vote was cast against him when he was elected President some year ago, notwithstanding the party divisions are just as acrimonious there, and more so than they are at the North—and cannot we be equally devoted? My friends, we must be; it is indispensable; and to do that we must treat each other with forbearance. If a man is loyal, whether he is an officer of the army, with whose success you have not been satisfied or a statesman with whom you have differed politically, if you believe his heart is right, you must not only refuse to assail him yourself, but discountenance forever, assaults upon him by anybody else. * * *

ONE CONSEQUENCE OF THE REBELLION.

What will be the end of this war in regard to one of the institutions which has been a subject of much discussion? I allude to Slavery. There have been great and delicate controversies on this subject heretofore. We have come now to a time when by the progress of our arms, Slavery is overthrown. By well-recognized principles of law it is as clear as the sun at noon, that if this war goes on twelve months there will not be a slave legally held in any one of the States and Territories, except by the President's proclamation. That is the necessary effect of the conquest of those States, and brought upon themselves by the war that they commenced.

THE PROSPECT BEFORE US.

I see nothing in the world to discourage any patriot, any friend of his country, any truly loyal man in the effort now making to uphold the authority of the Government, and to re-establish the Union and Constitution throughout the entire limits of the Country. I believe I know something of the people of this country; I think I ought to. I have been about with them for a large portion of my life, and I know that in every great crisis in the history of the country, the truly loyal men throughout the United States are disposed to uphold the Government and advance its honour. * * *

I don't believe—I never can be made to believe that this Government is to perish. What strikes me as the wicked feature in this rebellion, is that I know that if we had gone until to-day, such is the intelligence of our people, such their power, such their resources, that we should have been at this moment the first Power on the civilized globe; and I look forward to the time not far distant, when the authority of the Government shall be restored over the whole United States, and we shall again advance in a career of prosperity and of honour, without parallel in the history of the world.